Leicestershire
and the
First World War

Nick Miller

Title page: On 31 January 1916 nine Zeppelins set out from Germany, aiming to penetrate as far as Liverpool. Previous raids were confined to the East Coast and South East but this raid was designed to bring the war deep into home territory in order to hit morale, destroy industry and docks, and to demonstrate that no place in Britain was safe from attack. Snow, dense cloud and difficult navigation led to confusion amongst the airmen over their positions and they became scattered. Kapitänleutnant Franz Stabbert's L20 reached Loughborough at 20:00 hours, by some reports thinking it was Sheffield. Bombs fell on Orchard Street, the Rushes, and just missed Morris's engineering works. This picture shows a crowd viewing the crater in the yard of the Crown and Cushion, Ashby Square.

Text © Nick Miller, 2016.
First published in the United Kingdom, 2016,
by Stenlake Publishing Ltd.,
54-58 Mill Square,
Catrine, Ayrshire,
KA5 6RD
Telephone: 01290 551122
www.stenlake.co.uk

ISBN 9781840337600

The publishers regret that they cannot supply copies of any pictures featured in this book.

Acknowledgements

The photographs on pages 1 and 27, of the aftermath of the Zeppelin raid on Loughborough, are reproduced by kind permission of the Record Office for Leicestershire, Leicester & Rutland.

Introduction

From over 320 parishes in the county of Leicestershire only East Norton, Saxby and Stretton en le Field were 'Thankful Villages', a term popularised by writer Arthur Mee for communities that recorded no deaths in the Great War. The war stole more than 12,000 Leicestershire lives. The impact of the war, though, was broader than the tragic loss of life. For many, notably women, the very fabric of social and physical life transformed. There was the impact of the departure of fathers, sons, brothers, husbands, and sweethearts. Their duties and roles, though, still had to be performed, and it was women who widely took these on. Others, too, were called to duty – nurses, surgeons, road and railway workers, farmers, miners and factory staff switched to the war effort. Factories and fields became workshops of war.

In Leicester alone over 50 businesses converted to war work, amongst them prominent firms like British United Shoe Machinery Co. (BUSMC), Richards' Phoenix foundry, Goodwin Barsby, and Gimson's Vulcan engineering works. They switched peacetime industrial, agricultural and domestic appliance production for munitions, gun emplacements, and precision parts for weapons and machines. Gent's Faraday works manufactured signalling and telephone equipment, advanced technologies of the time; Taylor Hobson produced optical parts to replace the pre-war German sources for these. Even the Dryad factory with its iconic cane furniture switched to making shell baskets, balloon gondolas and nose-cones for aircraft.

Outside Leicester, Morris's Empress works and the Brush Falcon works in Loughborough retooled. Stableford's in Coalville turned out armoured wagons and shells. Iron-ore and coal mines upped output to supply the steelworks, railways and ships. Wright's in Quorn was a key producer of vital elastic. Home workers across the county created dressings and bandages for the front and for local hospitals.

Leicestershire had no dedicated military establishments like Woolwich Arsenal, no factories and workforce already geared to military production. All the factories had to restructure. Leicester led the nation in September 1915 when it was the first to deliver shells from factories transformed from peacetime roles. The system of local cooperation and sharing of expertise that achieved this was replicated as a model countrywide. Leicester was criticised at first for being slow and low to recruit – barely 3% in the early war compared to Derby's 5%, Nottingham's 18%, and Rutland's eventual 35%. But this partly reflected the high involvement of the town's population in war work, a factor that contributed to the government's post-war award of city status to Leicester.

Most local men enlisted in the Leicestershire Regiment (the Tigers; it did not attain the prefix of 'Royal' until 1946). Some were drafted to other regiments or the navy. Six Leicester lads perished alongside 1,260 others when HMS *Queen Mary* was destroyed at Jutland on 31 May 1916, and more were amongst the 1,929 lost in that same battle on HMS *Defence* and HMS *Invincible*. It was not just labourers who left. Families of the gentry like the Brooks and Martins sent and lost their sons. Sons of captains of industry were also killed, including those from the Corahs, Faires, Gimsons, Taylors and other families, in whose factories many of the other recruits' wives, sisters and mothers worked.

League rugby and cricket halted when hostilities commenced. Rugby international Kenneth Wood, and fellow rugby players A. McIntyre, William Dalby and others signed up. In May 1915 the Tigers' Welford Road ground became headquarters for the 176th (Leicester) Royal Artillery Howitzer Brigade (nicknamed 'Tigers Artillery'). Meanwhile, association football persisted and formal fixtures were only suspended after public and government pressure to stop. Poster campaigns were aimed at footballers with slogans like 'Play the Greater Game' and 'Make Khaki Your Colours'.

The Leicestershire and Rutland County Asylum next to Victoria Park became the Base Hospital of the 5th Northern War Hospital, the label given to the network of hospitals around Leicester (the Base Hospital was the main central one in terms of administration and number of beds). Cottage hospitals around the county such as at Lutterworth, Melton, Broome Leys and elsewhere admitted war wounded. Stately homes and halls were transformed to rehabilitation or convalescence stations – amongst them Wistow Hall, Cavendish Bridge and Admiral Beatty's Brooksby Hall.

Royal Army Medical Corps Territorial Force staff ran the Base Hospital. Many other groups were integral to its functioning, including laboratory staff and 202 Voluntary Aid Detachment (VAD) volunteers. Fifty-one nurses earned prestigious Royal Red Cross awards and other decorations, for example, Sister Dunne a silver Médaille des Epidémies du Ministère de la Guerre and Sister Wotherspoon the Samaritan Cross of Serbia. Nurse Marie Lufkin was a published war poet. Local people provided transport for patient outings, ran canteens and welcomed wounded into their homes for tea. They helped write letters – injuries prevented many from doing it themselves and it was also still an age of widespread illiteracy. People supplied reading materials, ran education classes, put on entertainment and organised sports. They helped with rehabilitation. Professions like physiotherapy (23 masseurs were employed; paraffin wax baths were prescribed) and speech therapy originated at this time. For example, Pte Albert Thomas of Clarendon Park, who was left with a stutter after his battle experiences, was likely to have been treated at the hospital for this condition. Occupational therapy was born from rehabilitation work in the hospital where basket-making was introduced, using wicker remnants from the Dryad works, leather offcuts from boot production, and embroidery from textile 'waste'.

Not everyone was swept by patriotism. Leicester MP Ramsay MacDonald, who in 1924 became the first Labour prime minister, opposed the war, at least to start with. Salvationist Councillor Amos Sherriff kept his pacifist principles: 'war belongs to the devil and everyone who supports it must claim the devil as a parent', he said on the outbreak of hostilities. Christian socialist Rev. Donaldson, vicar of St Mark's, Belgrave, and one of the leaders of the Leicester unemployed's landmark march to London in 1905, voiced similar disapproval. But their stance cost them. McDonald lost his seat because of it in the 1918 elections, along with Leicester Labour pacifist candidates Banton and Riley. The 'patriotic' wing of the Labour party blocked Sherriff from becoming the first Labour mayor of Leicester and Donaldson's anti-war stance is probably why the Church of England hierarchy denied him a bishopric.

The conflict impacted on those whose political, religious and moral beliefs saw the conflict as imperialist, capitalist, ungodly, inhuman and indefensibly wrong. Theirs was a forlorn voice with no sympathy in official circles and little amongst fellow citizens. Conscientious objectors (conchies) on religious grounds were still expected to join non-combat units. Those who resisted could expect similar consequences to political objectors – prison or delivery to the military where they could anticipate vindictive physical and mental abuse. Such was the fate of members of the Leicester Church of Christ on Crafton St (Mayor Jonathan North was a member of the congregation), who were imprisoned in Dartmoor. George Twilley, socialist and secretary of the No-Conscription Fellowship, was brutally beaten at Glen Parva barracks before imprisonment in Richmond, Durham, and Wormwood Scrubs.

Eli Bale, a Congregationalist preacher and draper from Kibworth Beauchamp, brother of well-known local photographer Walter Bale, disappeared. At his tribunal he had declared 'All through my life I have tried to be a follower of Christ and a Christian … I consider human life to be sacred, and under no circumstances would I take the same.' He had pleaded his one-man business would founder and his family be left destitute, and offered to undertake non-combatant war work. It seems he went on the run after his appeal was turned down. Others had more sway with the tribunal chairs. Captain Forrester, master of the Quorn hunt, gained exemption for a stable hand by maintaining that a healthy stock of horses was vital for the war.

As the war wore on, all was not united on the Home Front. Industrial unrest surfaced. Strikes were called at Mellor and Bromley's and Hart and Levy's, and later elsewhere, over the belief that refugees were receiving more pay than locals, workers on war contracts were earning more than civil workers, and the disparity between men's and women's wages. Unrest threatened to boil over into civil unrest from the activities of anti-war groups. The May Day rally in Leicester market place on 5 May 1918 was a case in point, when soldiers present tried to break through to seize Ramsay Macdonald and other speakers advocating peace. Others drowned out the speeches with shouting and singing 'God save the King' and fights between anti-war and 'patriotic' factions of the Labour movement also flared up. On other occasions shortages and mismanagement of distribution of food and other domestic supplies also provoked protests. Fuel rationing brought blackouts and heating cutbacks, and daylight saving stems from this time. Pubs closed at 9 p.m. – ostensibly to curb drunkenness amongst servicemen, but equally to conserve fuel.

On 11 November 1918 the bloodshed stopped, but the suffering of families who had lost loved ones did not. Political problems were far from solved and the ceasefire did not bring a halt to shortages, unemployment and hardship, all of which persisted into the 1920s and 30s. Outwardly in Leicestershire, as elsewhere, a new order in society emerged. Inwardly, the loss of loved ones remained raw. Commemorative gardens, windows and plaques appeared in clubs, churches, schools, factories and halls. More ambitious projects emerged. The world famous Loughborough carillon memorial was one. The Leicestershire Yeomanry column was built on Old John Hill in Bradgate Park to look down over the county towards homes the men had left. Bradgate Park was bought and donated to the people of Leicestershire in 1928 by Charles Bennion, managing director of BUSMC, one of whose sons suffered lifelong shell shock. The memorial arch in Leicester's Victoria Park, unveiled in 1925 and supported with funds from Mayor North, was designed by Sir Edwin Lutyens, designer of the Cenotaph in Whitehall, its form echoing that of the Menin Gate in Ypres.

Few recognise the largest project now as a war memorial. The intention had long been germinating to found a university in Leicester. As the war drew to a close this finally bore fruit, steered by the efforts of members of the Literary and Philosophical Society and other prominent political, business and medical personalities. Colonel Dr Astley Clarke, 5th Northern Hospital Administrator, William Brockington, County Director of Education, Captain (ear) surgeon Frederick Bennet, Rev. James Went and Dryad founder Harry Peach (all names of buildings now in Leicester's universities) instigated an appeal. Donations rapidly reached their target. Money flowed from families in memory of their fallen, while industrialists and organisations also contributed generously.

Thomas Fielding-Johnson, mill owner, Unitarian and local dignitary, whose grandson William had earned the Military Cross and bar in 1915 and 1918 (and Distinguished Flying Cross in 1942), secretly bought the 37-acre 5th Northern War Hospital site and buildings as a 'Peace Memorial worthy of our ancient Borough'. The buildings would serve as University College Leicester. It and the nearby new buildings for the Wyggeston girls' and boys' schools were to commemorate those who sacrificed their chance to learn, but secured that privilege for future generations. The committee took as their lead the passage of the Good Shepherd from Chapter 10 of St John's Gospel. Like war, 'The thief comes only to steal, and to kill, and to destroy'. But 'I am come that they may have life, and in abundance'. The university's motto is *Ut vitam habeant* – 'That they may have life'.

The band of the 1st Leicestershire Regiment playing at Glen Parva barracks in more leisurely pre-war times. The barracks were completed in 1880. Originally intended for 500 men, they became the home and training ground for thousands of recruits, both local and from wider afield. Overflow recruits were billeted with local families and in halls, schools and camps around Wigston and Oadby.

Magazine barracks, Leicester. Richard III most likely rode out to battle through this archway of Leicester Castle on 21 August 1485 to meet defeat and death at the fateful battle of Bosworth the next day. Later this was the home of the Leicestershire Militia and, with new buildings added in the nineteenth century, subsequently became headquarters of the Leicestershire Regiment.

MEN OF LEICESTERSHIRE

AVENGE THE LUSITANIA

HOW TO DO IT!

For every Man, Woman and Child lost 10 Men should join.

JOIN THE 10TH BATTALION LEICESTERSHIRE REGIMENT
21, HUMBERSTONE GATE.

14 DAYS LEAVE AT HOME ON JOINING

PAY AND ALLOWANCES **3/- PER DAY** WHILST ON LEAVE.

The Cunard liner *Lusitania* was torpedoed on 7 May 1915 by U-Boot U20 off Kinsale Head, Ireland. 1,194 people perished, sparking countrywide riots and attacks on German shopkeepers and residents. In Leicestershire the disturbances were minor compared to other cities. The high feelings around the sinking, though, were exploited as a call to arms. This poster urges revenge by enlisting for the 10th Leicesters, a training battalion which prepared men at home before sending them off to the 6th–9th Tigers battalions for combat.

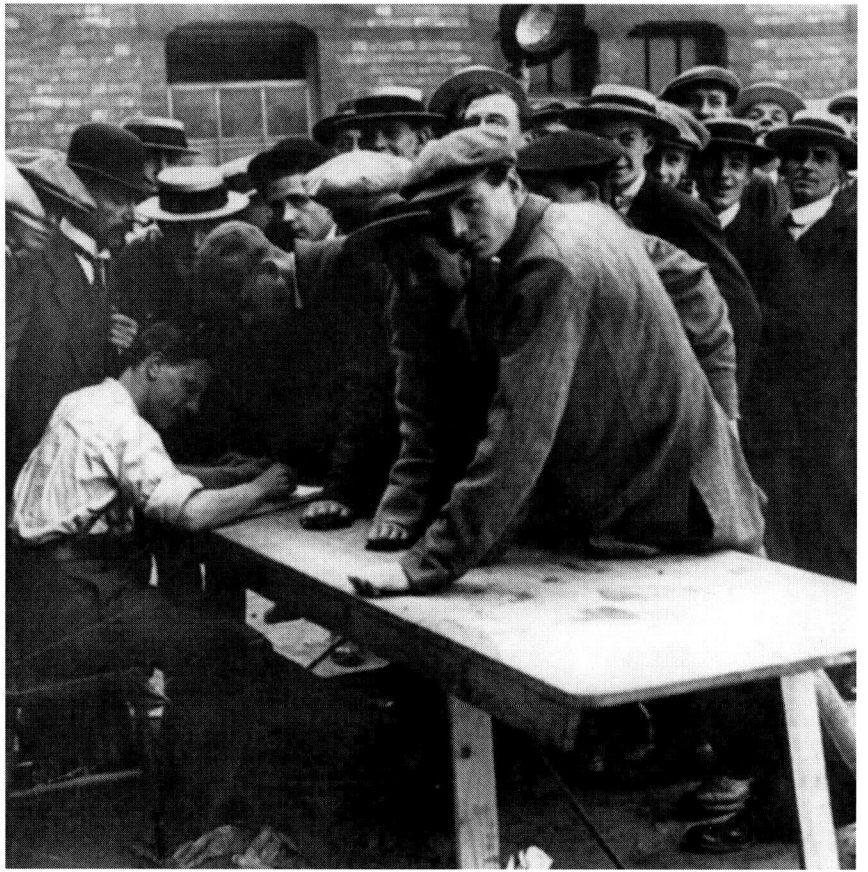

Eager recruits signing up in September 1914 in the Magazine barracks square.

The 5th Leicesters assembling for departure at Loughborough, August 1914. They would fight at Lens, Vimy, Kemmel, Gommecourt, Cambrai, Hill 70 and elsewhere. They experienced the first 'liquid fire' (flamethrower) attack on the British at Hooge on 30 July 1915. A report in their battalion history relates the story of a remarkable warning which was thrown over from the German lines to their trench, tied to a stone: 'We are going to send a 40lb bomb. We have got to do it, but don't want to. It will come this evening, and we will whistle first to warn you.'

Army stable hands at Stoughton, by Leicester postcard photographer Thomas Moore. He had started working life as a bricklayer and retained an interest in working life scenes after taking up photography professionally. Horses played a central role in the war, for transport of men and goods and motive power for wagons, canons and machinery. Grooms tended the bridles, reins and harnesses vital for towing gear. More farriers were based at Oadby Racecourse near to Glen Parva barracks.

Another Thomas Moore shot, this time of farriers at Oadby in 1916. In 1914 hundreds of local horses were requisitioned and assembled in cattle markets around the county. Local coal, baker, butcher and other delivery services protested they were unable to deliver their goods, but to no avail – the war took precedence.

Leicestershire Yeomanry C Section mobilising at Loughborough market place, 6 August 1914. They were led out from here to Grantham and onwards by Boer war veteran Major William Martin, of the local Mountsorrel Granite Company family. On 13 May 1915, at the Battle of Frezenberg, Martin died in the same trench as fellow yeomen Major Bernard Liebert, Lt. Teddy Brooks, Lt. Colin Peake, Sgt. Lionel Burton and Troopers Matthew Hickling, from Syston, and Charles Adams from Quorn. Eighty-seven others from C Section died that day.

Loughborough Midland station, with the Brush engineering factory in the background, as shown on a postcard that was posted on 6 October 1914. The recruits are clutching their new kit and were headed to Glen Parva barracks at Wigston. Jim (cross, right back) notes in the postcard's message, written from the barracks: 'We do not look so spick and span now as we did then.'

Not all Leicesters (the Tigers) came from Leicestershire. Recruits could be assigned virtually anywhere where numbers needed to be made up or where their skills could be exploited. Equally, not all recruits from Leicestershire joined the Tigers. This card by Parker Herbert, Hinckley, honouring early recruits from Earl Shilton illustrates the variety of destinations even from one parish. Sailors Alfred Armstrong, 31, and Arthur Clarke, 23, died on HMS *Black Prince* and HMS *Queen Mary* at the Battle of Jutland on 31 May 1916. J. Ladkin survived the near destruction of HMS *Acasta* that day. W. Bray (killed, 24 September 1914) and W. Green (killed, 17 October 1914), husband of Earl Shilton's postmistress Gertrude, fell even before the postcard was published.

Leicester National Reserves, 7 Section, No. 1 Company, ready to board the train for duty. National Reserves were men who had seen previous military service but had left the army. Depending on how long ago this was, and on age, fitness and experience, they were either assigned to guarding key installations in Britain or abroad, for example in Egypt or India, or given training roles or consigned to regular battalions.

Photo by Ramsden, Leicester.

A happy batch of splendid Leeds Lads billeted at the Leicester Y.M.C.A. taking Dinner in the "Hut."—May 18th, 1916.

The war saw a constant toing and froing of men. Here, 'a happy batch of splendid Leeds lads', who stopped off at London Road station on 18 May 1916 en route south, are dining at Leicester's Young Men's Christian Association (YMCA, called by some 'Your Memory Clings Always'). Apart from billeting, the YMCA also provided canteens, entertainment (see page 35), and spiritual support. The photographer was J. Ramsden of Granby Street, whose premises at 63 Granby Street were practically next door to the YMCA.

The county cricket ground on Leicester's Aylestone Road was used for exercising, as a rifle range, and as the HQ of several military and support groups. The picture shows a Sunday service of Citizen Volunteers in 1915 and appears on a postcard sent by Sidney Packer of Upperton Road, who was quartermaster of the Leicester Volunteer Battalion and the secretary of Leicester Rugby Union who lent the Tigers' ground for war purposes. Over 40 cricketers and ground staff enlisted. Harold Wright, wicket keeper Arthur Davies, Albert Shipman, Joseph Surman, William Odell (who in his debut game had bowled the legendary W.G. Grace) all died. W. Riley lost a leg, later becoming inspector of propellants at Woolwich Arsenal.

The 1913–14 Leicester Fosse team. Nicknamed the Fossils, they did not become City until 1919. Their final regular match was on 24 April 1915, against Clapton (later Leyton) Orient, who at the final whistle changed into khaki kit and marched off to war. Football and cricket star Arthur Mounteney and over 50 current or former Fosse players joined up. Eleven died, including Tommy Benfield (front row, first in on the right), the top scorer in the 1913–14 season. He had been the first to score in Arsenal's new Highbury Stadium and was killed by a sniper in September 1918.

Arnold Shuttlewood (seated third from right) of Sileby, later Syston, and after the war a farm labourer in Syston, enlisted in the Royal Field Artillery in 1917. He followed his brothers to France and was later posted to Ireland.

The Aliens Restriction Act of September 1914 targeted suspected enemy sympathisers and many Germans and Austrians were interned. In Leicestershire, as elsewhere, there were excesses, with shops looted and people driven out, sometimes simply for having a German sounding name. On 7 August 1914 Germans and Austrians were imprisoned at gun point and locked up in Leicester's Corn Exchange until they could be transferred to internment camps. One casualty was Edwin Wildt whose family owned the Adelaide hosiery machinery factory in the Newarkes, which at the time was switching to war work. To avoid internment he fled to the USA and set up a successful factory there. Others around the county suffered too, including Carl Namegah, upholsterer of Wartnaby Street, Market Harborough. The owner of Kunzle's pâtisserie, 37 Market Street, Leicester, was actually Swiss and from Birmingham; nevertheless, because of his German sounding name, his premises seem to have been boarded up through the war to avoid trouble. Butcher George Leeson of 117 King Richards Road, Leicester, was also attacked by crowds in May 1915 after the sinking of the *Lusitania* simply because it was rumoured he had visited Germany.

Anti-German feeling persisted, right down to street names. Who today walks down Leicester's Beaconsfield Road and Gotham, Saxby, Severn and Andover streets and knows they were Bismarck, Gotha, Saxe-Coburg, Mecklenburg and Hannover streets until 1918? The Blücher pub on Wellington Street, Leicester, was renamed the Admiral Beatty, after the supposed victor at Jutland 1916; an ironic twist of fate, given that it was the arrival of Blücher's army at Waterloo in 1815 that saved the British. Brunswick Street and Battenberg Street remained unchanged, unlike the aristocratic family who adopted the name Mountbatten.

Brush Falcon works, Loughborough, which had over 2,000 workers, switched from electrical engineering and building trams, to manufacturing munitions, vehicle bodies, planes and rolling stock for the narrow gauge railways behind the fronts (one is just visible on page 25). Over 1,300 women were trained for work at Brush and other Loughborough factories at a dedicated wartime instructional centre at the town's Technical School (years later to become Loughborough University). Amongst skills acquired were gauge making, technical design, pattern making and aero-engine testing.

British United Shoe Machinery Company (BUSMC), Leicester, the world's largest manufacturer of boot and shoe machinery, employed over 4,000 workers. Over 800 of its men joined up and were replaced by women. It moved to shell production, but also made fuses, naval gun mountings, aeroplane engine and other precision parts. The message on the postcard on the left records the factory was by then doing war work and stretched back along all the local streets.

Naval gun emplacements produced at BUSMC, waiting for shipment.

Women at a Leicester factory, wearing their OWS (On War Service) badges. These were first issued to men to show they were in vital war work, not avoiding enlistment. In 1916, after wider conscription, the Ministry of Munitions issued the triangular pin badge exclusively to women war workers. Here it looks like the women formed not just the labour force but the cricket team as well.

Textile, hosiery and boot and shoe industries adapted too. Fielding-Johnson's supplied more yarn for military purposes than any other firm in the country; Corah's turned out over 10 million clothing items during the war; and the Wheatsheaf Works, Equity, Freeman Hardy Willis', Lennards' and others produced gaiters, webbing, the boots that trod the trenches, and belts that drove engines. This 1918 photograph, another from Thomas Moore, shows staff of the Co-op Wheatsheaf Boot and Shoe Factory, Knighton.

A *Daily Mail* official war card of the Leicesters, showing 'Tommy as a picture of contentment'. Recently of Boer War siege of Ladysmith renown, the Tigers had fought in India, the Crimean War, the Peninsular War, Afghanistan and more. Now new names were added to their colours, unfamiliar to most today, but for county folk then they tripped off the tongue with sad ease: Neuve Chappelle, Rue du Bois, La Houssoie, the Hohenzollern Redoubt, Mametz, Bazentin, Scherpenberg, Pontruet, Épehy.

Machine guns captured by the 2nd Leicesters in a night attack on 19 December 1914 near Richebourg L'Avoue. This photograph appeared on a postcard written in July 1915 from Nell, of 48 King Richard's Road, Leicester, to Cis Tilbury of 30 Churchill Street. The 2nd Battalion and Indian Garhwal Brigade fought in France before transfer in December 1915 to Mesopotamia (which was jokingly but cynically labelled 'Mess-up Otania'). They endured battles and disease along the Tigris, led the march into Baghdad in 1917, then moved to Palestine and ended the war at the Battle of Megiddo.

After the Zeppelin raid on Loughborough on 31 January 1916 crowds came to view the spectacle. Some folk in Anstey were given the day off and cycled over. This photograph shows The Rushes, with the Blue Boar pub on the right and the Rising Sun lodging house next door. Arthur Turnill, 50, father of 12, recently married Joseph and Alice Adkin, Mary Page and her teenage children, and four others died in the bombing.

Wood's woollen factory, founded 1755, was built on east Leicestershire sheep farming. It was renamed 'Wolsey's' in 1897, commemorating Cardinal Wolsey who died on 29 November 1530 at Leicester Abbey, next door to the factory. Wolsey's supplied garments to both Scott and Amundsen on their 1911–12 South Pole expeditions. Between 1914–18 they supplied 14 million garments for the government. Here a Wolsey's lorry is fundraising for VAD (Voluntary Aid Detachments).

A VAD reception, most likely at Leicester Midland station. The commandant was Mrs L. Taylor. Military personnel arriving in Leicester or changing trains there could get free food, drinks and smokes. Attending the reception, but not seen in this picture (by J. Ramsden), is Pte W. Buckingham. In 1915 he won a VC near Neuve Chapelle for 'bravery and devotion to duty in rescuing and rendering aid … whilst exposed to heavy fire'. He tended a wounded German soldier as well as British comrades. A bullet that would have killed him was deflected by a pack of postcards and a cartridge case in his breast pocket. After treatment he toured recruitment rallies around Leicestershire. He died on the Somme on 15 September 1916, his body never recovered.

A fundraising gala at Spence Street baths, Leicester. The men are wearing the blue trousers and jacket, red tie and white shirt uniform that distinguished wounded servicemen. A joke of the time, since the uniforms seldom fitted, was writing home to report a 'bad fit of the blues'.

Meeting wounded at Leicester Midland station to bring them to the 5th Northern General War Hospital (now Leicester University). Hospital trains arrived at the milk and parcels sidings to give access to ambulances and not disrupt normal traffic. Convoys arrived all hours of the day and night. The first admission to the hospital was on 1 September 1914; the first convoy of wounded (127 of them) arrived on 2 September 1914. The first death occurred on 4 September 1914 – Pte W Hodges. This card posted on 27 September 1914 may show the first contingent arriving. Between then and the arrival of the last convoy on 8 June 1919, 425 convoy trains were received.

With over 5,000 beds at its peak, the 5th Northern War Hospital was the fourth largest in the country after Liverpool, Birmingham and Manchester. By comparison even today's super hospitals offer only around 1,000 beds and most district general hospitals between 300 and 400. The Base Hospital recorded almost 75,000 patients (nearer 100,000 with the 61 auxiliary sites). They included 2,503 Canadians, 1,057 Australians and New Zealanders, 433 Belgians and 59 Germans/Austrians. Some wards – like ward J2 here, showing Sister Ecott (front left) – had open air facilities for those suffering respiratory problems from gas attacks.

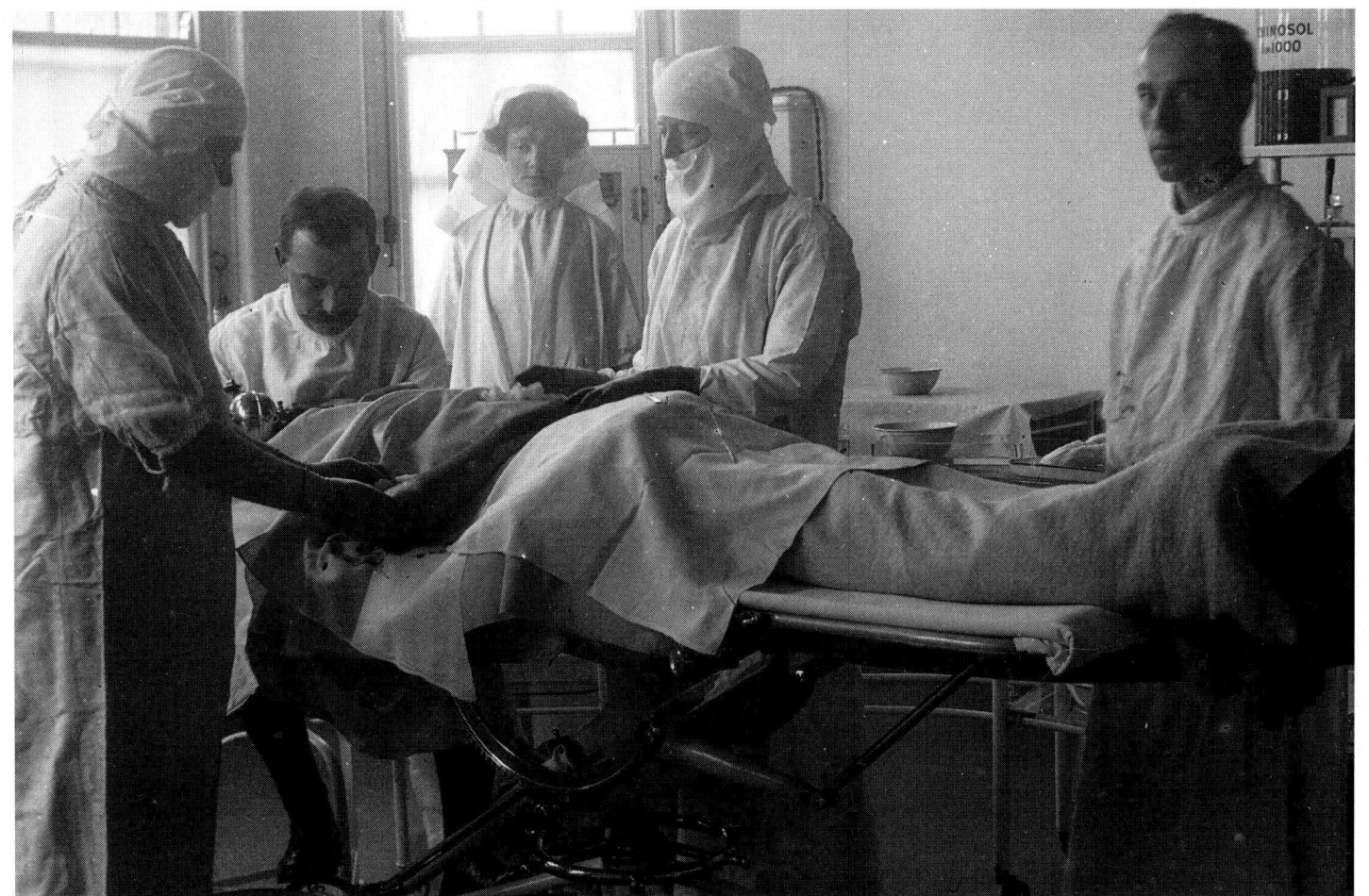

There was first aid at the front, if a soldier was lucky, and treatment stations just behind the lines. Lifesaving operations were conducted in field hospitals and further operations, care and rehabilitation took place back in Britain. This scene at the Base Hospital by postcard photographer Moore shows one such operation underway. During the war 7,808 operations were performed at the Base Hospital alone. Around 75,000 patients passed through, and of these 54,111 were discharged back to leave and duty. Only 514 deaths were recorded, less than 0.7% of admissions, a remarkable achievement. Alas the most seriously wounded usually died before repatriation. The hospital provided outpatient services too. Medical staff examined over 10,000 recruits at Glen Parva barracks. The ophthalmic centre dispensed 3,453 pairs of spectacles.

The Base Hospital, most likely H ward, Christmas 1915. Sister Birch stands by the pillar. Staff Nurse G. Lewis, later decorated with the Royal Red Cross medal, is centre back. To her left stands Surgeon Captain Robert Fagge of Melton. The photographer was Herbert Wilson of Market Street.

The North Evington Poor Law Infirmary was designated the Evington War Hospital in March 1915. Today it's the Leicester General. Patients are posing outside wards 1 and 3. The picture by Timson of Leicester was passed by the Government Press Bureau censor on 13 October 1916 and appeared on a postcard send from Jim Scott in 1918 to his wife, who lived at 29 Cavendish Road, Newcastle. He was being treated for abscesses on infected wounds and was writing whilst drinking a cup of tea at the YMCA, just having won five shillings!

Shells and bullets wrought death and injury, but in pre-antibiotic days wound infections and primitive and overcrowded living conditions could kill. Pneumonia, dysentery, TB, wet gangrene, typhoid, malaria and tetanus all took their toll. Here soldiers at Leicester Gilroes Isolation Hospital, probably the TB ward (despite the cigarettes!) pose with some of their nurses.

Mental restoration was integral to rehabilitation. The card shows men and nurses on D1 ward of the Base Hospital in January 1915. Locals donated indoor games (more than 2,000), 23 billiard tables (there were inter-ward competitions), pianos, 66 gramophones, 5,070 78 rpm records and 350,000 styluses for them. They also provided tobacco (more than 12,000lb), and 12 million cigarettes. Each patient received 40 cigarettes or 2oz. tobacco per week from the hospital.

Town Hall Square, Leicester, 1918. The tank was nicknamed 'Ole Bill' after the famous character, whose catchphrase was 'if you can find a better 'ole, go to it', who featured weekly in 'Fragments from France', a cartoon feature that appeared in *The Bystander*, a popular tabloid magazine of the time. The tank promoted fundraising for government war bonds. There was inter-town rivalry for who could raise the most. The Leicester War Savings Committee aimed to beat Birmingham's total. They did easily, with way over £2 million for the week.

The picture shows Ben Tillett, trade unionist, Fabian Society member, co-founder of the Independent Labour Party, and MP for Salford North from 1917–24, addressing the crowds from 'Ole Bill'. He had professed pacifism before the war but was amongst those in the labour movement who, when it came to war, supported military action. In a pamphlet Tillett justified his stance by claiming, 'We realised that this is a fight for world freedom against a carefully engineered plan to establish a world autocracy'.

Sentry Box and Entanglements, Donington Hall.

Castle Donington Hall dated from the middle ages but was rebuilt in the 1790s for Rawdon-Hastings, the 2nd Earl of Moira, military commander, and colonial governor. It was requisitioned in 1914 and converted to a maximum security officers' POW camp. It had double wire fences (the inner one electrified), searchlights and traps. Inside, though, officers lived in relative luxury – they had dining rooms, amusements, sports, and even a cash allowance transferred from Germany.

Officers arrived at Castle Donington on Fridays, this group on 7 July 1916. Intended for 500 to 600 POWs, mostly about 120 were housed there. One was Kapitänleutnant Gunther Plüschow, air ace and adventurer, who would die in 1931 on a pioneering flight in the southern Andes. Having evaded capture when Japanese and British forces overran the German colony of Tsingtao in China in November 1914, he had made his way to San Francisco, then New York. From there he took a boat bound for Italy, but was arrested when the ship had to dock in Gibraltar. He described in his autobiography arriving at Donington in May 1915 to a 'howling mob of women and … undersized children … The women and the girls … behaved like savages. Yelling and whistling … occasional stones and clods of earth', but most 'splitting with laughter at the antics'. Plüschow soon planned his escape. Having gleaned from guards where they were and how to get to Derby, he and fellow officer Oskar Trefftz hid under garden furniture to await their opportunity. They cut through the entanglements during a storm on 4 July 1915. Their absence was covered by comrades reporting them sick and others pretending to be them in their beds when the guards checked. The plan was hatched when they saw a fawn get in through the fence and they realised it was not impregnable.

Guards lining up for duty at Donington POW camp. On escaping, Trefftz made it as far as Millwall docks before he was arrested, but Plüschow walked to Derby and took a train to London. There he hid, amongst other places, in the British Museum and bluffed his way for several days around the city. He ascertained news of a boat crossing the North Sea and swam out in the Thames at Tilbury to the Dutch steamer Princes Juliana which was heading back to the Netherlands. He was the only POW in either world war to make a successful home run from Britain.

Sgt. Jack Harding (back row, 2nd right), of 71 Clifford Street, Wigston, was a soldier in the 1st Leicesters. He was held in barrack 47 at Göttingen POW camp. He worked on advertising in the camp newspaper, *The Wooden City*. Other Leicesters helping to edit and write it included Sgt. D. Shea, CSM H. Connors (he shared barrack 41a with Harding) and Pte R. Ellis. Sgt. C. Hickman was on the amusements committee. CQM Sgt. McCarthy arranged boxing tournaments. Two prominent boxers were Leicesters – Privates Dodge and McGuire.

A view of Göttingen camp, with prisoners on duties. Leicesters were housed there with up to 10,000 Russian, French, Belgian and other British military, and also civilians from occupied lands. Among the Leicesters who passed through were J. Allen, R. Camp, F. Chambers, F. Cliff, T. Dawkes, H. Fall, H. Green, A. Hall, G. Hunter, A. Iliffe, P. Keane, G. Lee, E. Lomas, L. McCarthy, G. Naylor, H. Ormes, P. Pallett, ? Ratcliffe, J. Tinkler, G. Todd, A. Vokins and E. Woolford.

Jack Taylor (back, cross) was in the 4th Leicesters and this picture was taken in Friedrichsfeld bei Wesel POW camp. The card is from his father to the Leicester POW Committee, which posted food and other goods to prisoners. His message sends grateful thanks to the committee for its generous support for his son. The Leicestershire POW committee dispatched provisions to county men and, amongst other things, sent over 20 tons of sugar, 12 tons of tea, a ton of cocoa and over 4 million cigarettes.

The National Society of Operative Printers' Assistants (NATSOPA) Memorial Homes, chapel and gardens, commemorating printers who fell in the war. It was situated at Wellsborough, Market Bosworth, opening in 1921 as convalescent homes. It was sold to the Pilgrim's Friend Society in the 1960s and later became the Hornsey Rise Home. When it closed in 2013 it was left to dilapidation and fell prey to copper and fittings thieves.

The Loughborough carillon (local folk say 'carillion') bells, heading down Freehold Street in 1923. The tower was fashioned after the bell towers in Flanders. Henrietta Godber of 10 Thomas Street, laid the foundation stone as representative for 480 families of the town's fallen. Her stretcher bearer son Billy, 2/5th Leicesters, died carrying a comrade back to safety on 16 April 1917. The 47 bells were cast in Taylor's (three of his four sons died) world famous bell foundry. The girders were made at Morris's Empress works. The bricks came from Gilbert Tucker's Great Central brick works.

In Memory of Leicester's Fallen Heroes, 1914 - 1917.

The interim memorial unveiled on 28 June 1917 at Leicester Town Hall Square, next to the Boer War memorial. As one of the spurs for erecting the interim memorial mayor Jonathan North declared, 'a desire to acknowledge public grief' and 'bring home to many people, especially young people, who seem to be still regarding the war with indifference, the seriousness of the times in which they live'. Its designers were S. Pick of Everard & Pick and B. Fletcher, head of Leicester's School of Art. The builders were H. Herbert's, Millstone Lane. The plasterer was A. Crewe of Newfoundpool. J. Morcom was the sculptor, from Kirby Muxloe (he also made the memorial there). 2,129 names were listed under the inscription, 'They did not fail us: we must not fail them'. The council did: after Victoria Park memorial opened in 1925, 29 years of neglect of the interim memorial ended in an act of council vandalism with its demolition in April 1954.